Incredible Explorers

Hernán Cortés
Conquering the Aztec Empire

Zachary Anderson

Cavendish Square

New York

Published in 2015 by Cavendish Square Publishing, LLC
243 5th Avenue, Suite 136, New York, NY 10016

Library of Congress Cataloging-in-Publication Data

Anderson, Zachary.
Hernán Cortés : Conquering the Aztec Empire / Zachary Anderson.
pages cm. — (Incredible explorers)
Includes index.
ISBN 978-1-50260-129-2 (hardcover) ISBN 978-1-50260-130-8 (ebook)
1. Cortés, Hernán, 1485-1547—Juvenile literature. 2. Mexico—History—Conquest, 1519-1540—Juvenile literature.
3. Mexico—Discovery and exploration—Spanish—Juvenile literature. 4. Conquerors—Mexico—Biography—Juvenile
literature. 5. Explorers—Mexico—Biography—Juvenile literature. 6. Explorers—Spain—Biography—Juvenile literature.
I. Title.

F1230.C35R36 2015
972.02092—dc23
[B]

2014025531

Editor: Andrew Coddington
Copy Editor: Cynthia Roby
Art Director: Jeffrey Talbot
Designer: Douglas Brooks
Senior Production Manager: Jennifer Ryder-Talbot
Production Editor: David McNamara
Photo Researcher: J8 Media

Contents

The Supreme Conquistador

 ernán Cortés was more than just another hungry Spaniard who had ventured across the Atlantic to **Hispaniola** or Cuba, or any of the isles in the Caribbean that Spain claimed. Those were men in search of great

Hernán Cortés is remembered as one of history's greatest and most controversial explorers.

fortune. They wanted to make a name for themselves and be the pride of their families back in Europe. There were scores of them, all looking for money and hoping to gain land and titles. Few of those men, however, were true explorers. Genuine explorers had to be leaders who were prepared for the unknown and able to act decisively. Of all the **New World** adventurers whose names are recorded for posterity, whether English, Portuguese, French, or Spanish, Cortés was the one who first pushed through to the center of a great, unknown civilization, truly walked upon the land, and led the conquest for two continents.

Few events have affected the world as much as the discovery and subsequent conquest of the Americas. Some obvious changes came forth after 1492, such as the mingling of varied indigenous and European cultures and the merging of once-distant peoples, which brought on a new era of slavery, disease, and genocide. Other changes were more subtle, but no less important. These included the introduction of plant and animal life from North America to Europe, as well as the introduction of new foods, such as tomatoes, corn, and chocolate, to the once-bland European diet.

Spain had been largely responsible for this burst of worldwide exploration, so its leaders would probably have inevitably instigated a conflict with the Native people of the Americas during the sixteenth century. Under Cortés's dynamic leadership, though, the conquest took place with more speed and simplicity than Spain had thought possible. Cortés was a gambler who took risks, and with those risks he gained enormous ground. His boastful nature helped him forge a path few men could follow.

Reading about the life of Cortés, one is struck by the contradictions in his interactions in the New World. While he claimed to be an ardent follower of Christianity, his brutal conquering

Though he was born into poor circumstances, Hernán Cortés would go on to conquer one of the greatest civilizations in the New World.

of the **Aztec** people does not match the teachings of that faith. While he claimed to be advancing the cause of his nation Spain, he was willing to attack his own countrymen to keep what he'd seized. Finally, if his goal was wealth and power, he could have easily settled down with the riches he'd accumulated, yet he continued to explore and conquer right up until his death. His actions would change the course of history for generations living in both the Old World and the New.

Hernán Cortés

Chapter 1

A New Conquest for a New World

he Spanish Empire fought a protracted war with the **Moors** (Muslims) for centuries. The Moors quickly gained the upper hand in the 700s CE. It was then that they conquered the Spanish Empire, as well as North Africa, parts

The Islamic Moors ruled Spain for more than 700 years. They left a mark on the country's history, as evidenced by the ruins of Costa del Sol, an Islamic castle in southern Spain.

of the Indian subcontinent, Persia, Greece, and Turkey. Despite the geographic difficulties of controlling such a wide area, for 700 years the Moors spread their Islamic faith throughout parts of Europe, including Spain.

The response to this invasion was a long series of wars known as the *Reconquista*, or the Reconquest. Gradually whittling away at the Moorish regions of Spain, the Christian kingdoms slowly expanded back across the **Iberian Peninsula**. In this religious clash between Christianity and **Islam**, tensions were high on both sides. For the Spanish, the Reconquest became more than a patriotic struggle against an invader; it became a holy war, ordered by God. The Spanish wanted to drive all the **infidels**, or nonbelievers, out of Spain in God's name.

The Muslims who were conquered by the Spanish were often made to suffer and were forced, sometimes violently, to convert to Christianity. The intolerance of the Spanish toward the Moors was also extended to other non-Christian peoples, especially the Jews, who had found a refuge in Moorish Spain and had helped to make that region one of the most enlightened sections in all of Europe. This intolerance of other religions became an important characteristic of Spanish explorers' attitudes toward the Native peoples they would meet throughout the New World.

Exploring Two New Continents

In 1492, the last Moorish region in Spain was finally reconquered. That same year, a Genoese navigator sailed from Palos, Spain, with the support of the Spanish Crown. This man, Christopher Columbus, believed that the world was much smaller than his contemporaries thought. Therefore, he also firmly believed that reaching the East Indies could be accomplished more quickly by sailing west from Europe rather than around the tip of Africa, as

Christopher Columbus was the first European to discover the West Indies and its riches, laying the groundwork for intense European activity in that area.

the Portuguese believed. Although he was wrong about reaching the East Indies, he did find lands that would one day make Spain the richest kingdom in Europe.

Columbus, despite the fact that he truly believed he had reached the islands that bordered the coast of Asia, had not "discovered" the Americas either. The land was already inhabited by millions of Native Americans when he began exploring the Caribbean Islands.

The Central and South American empires were remarkably sophisticated, especially when one considers that there were no animals such as horses available in the Americas. Moreover, before the Europeans arrived, the Mayan, Incan, and Aztec cultures had not grasped the importance of the wheel as a tool. In the coming clash of civilizations, the accomplishments of cultures hundreds of years old were to be swept away by the guns, horses, and steel of the Spanish.

Into this world of rapid change and conflict was born Hernán Cortés. (His name is often spelled Hernando, Fernan, or even Fernando, which are all more or less the same in Spanish; his last name is sometimes given as Cortez.) He was born in 1485, in the town of Medellin in Extremadura, one of the poorest sections of Spain. His father, Martin Cortés, was a poor landowner. However, Martin was able to claim the title of *hidalgo*, or gentleman. Although not a noble, like a count or duke, he was above the common people even if he was poor. Unlike nobles, Martin Cortés had only pride to pass on to his son.

A Difficult Childhood

Because he was very sickly, Hernán Cortés was not expected to survive past childhood. **Last rites**, or final prayers of absolution in the Christian religion, were said over the boy several times. Over time, though, he grew to be a strong young man and an excellent horseman and swordfighter. He also developed his mind.

When he was fourteen years of age (or so he would later claim), he was sent by his parents to attend Salamanca, the greatest university in Spain, to become a lawyer. Whether or not he actually went, Cortés never earned a degree. (Some historians have speculated that he merely served as a clerk to a lawyer.) It is known, however, that he could read and write in both Spanish and Latin. He had at least a basic grasp of the complex Spanish legal system. This knowledge of the law would later serve him well during his conquest of Mexico.

For whatever reason, Cortés returned home from school after only two years. The sixteen-year-old boy was now a rebellious young man. His unruly attitude led his parents to decide that it would be best if he left their house and found his own way in the world.

Cortés studied law at the prestigious University of Salamanca, though he never received a degree.

Setting Out For the New World

At this point, during the early sixteenth century, there were two paths that a young Spaniard might choose. One was to go to Italy and join the Spanish war against the French being waged there. The other was to follow Columbus's path to the New World and the tiny Spanish colonies in the Caribbean Islands. The islands had proved to be disappointing in some ways. They were certainly not the Moluccas, or Spice Islands, of the East Indies that were the original goal of Columbus. They did, however, offer tantalizing hints of wealth to come, especially in gold. The Spanish adventurers, known as *conquistadors,* often returned from the New World to Spain wearing golden ornaments, a sign of what future exploration of the region might bring.

The choice was easy for Cortés. He would travel to the New World in search of riches and new lands. In the end, however, his voyage was put on hold. The cause of his delay was a woman, for the young Cortés had become well known for having relation-ships with many different women. One night, while walking along the top of a wall returning from meeting a married woman, the wall crumbled beneath his feet and he fell into a garden. He was badly injured and soon fell ill. The fleet his parents had arranged for him to sail with to the New World departed without him.

When he had recovered from his injuries and illness, Cortés decided he would go to Italy instead of the West Indies. His parents raised the money for this trip as well. Once again, he did not go. Instead, Cortés wandered around Spain, often penniless and hungry. Without direction in his life, his original idea of traveling to the New World in search of easy money must have begun to look better. Eventually, he returned to Medellin and begged his parents once more for the money to sail to the New World. Perhaps glad to finally be rid of their rebellious son, they were able to gather enough money to send Cortés across the ocean to Hispaniola, the main Spanish colony in the West Indies.

Reaching Hispaniola

Cortés's sea voyage was a miserable one. The captain of his ship tried to beat the rest of the fleet across the ocean, only to get completely lost. Nearly starving and almost out of water, the ship's crew finally sighted a white dove, a bird that could only have come from land. It was Good Friday in the year 1504. Two days later, on Easter Sunday, Cortés landed in the New World.

At nineteen years of age, Cortés arrived in Santo Domingo, the town founded by Columbus in Hispaniola and the center of the Spanish Empire in the West Indies. He was poor, but in Hispaniola even a poor man could live like a lord, or so it seemed.

The *Encomienda* System

Thanks to the *encomienda* system, Cortés was granted a small parcel of land, and indigenous people who were forced to farm it in return for being fed and taught about Christianity (something the Native people had not asked for). Cortés was told that if he stayed with his land for five years he would own it. This infamous Spanish practice was designed as an alternative to outright slavery. This system was little better, and often worse, than slavery, as the Spanish often cruelly mistreated the Native people.

At the time, Cortés had no intention of staying anywhere in the New World for as long as five years, as he told the clerk who assigned him his land. Yet he was, in fact, fated to stay there for seven long years as an obscure colonist with nothing to mark him as exceptional.

Cortés remained a wild, impulsive, and sometimes even violent young man. He had frequent affairs with the women native to the island, and entered into at least one duel, a sword fight that left him scarred on his chin. It was a mark he later covered with a beard. At the same time, Cortés found more respectable work acting as a notary public (a public position requiring some knowledge of the law) in the village of Azua, about 50 miles (80.5 kilometers) from Santo Domingo.

A Prophetic Dream

Toward the end of this period, Cortés is said to have had an unusual dream. In it he was surrounded by strange people who addressed him with great reverence. He was wearing rich garments and was in an obvious position of honor and respect. When he told other people about his dream, it seemed like a prophecy of things to come.

In 1511, the twenty-six-year-old Cortés made his first move to establish a name for himself in the New World. An expedition was being organized to conquer the nearby island of Cuba, and Cortés served as a secretary to its commander, Diego Velázquez. Velázquez was one of the original settlers of Santo Domingo and a veteran of Spain's many wars. He had become one of the most important men in Hispaniola, founding several towns. A man known to have been mild-mannered, Velázquez was also a devious politician and ruthless commander.

Velázquez had ordered the massacre of many of the peaceful Native people of Hispaniola, and he did likewise in Cuba, where there was little resistance to the Spanish invasion. He also tried to use the expedition to grab more land and glory for himself. Cortés, who became close to Velázquez, observed his behavior firsthand, and may have learned many lessons from the older, more experienced man. He may, however, have learned a bit too well.

The movement to Cuba was just the first step toward a set of significant changes that would reshape the future of both the Old World and the New World. While Cortés would find success (and some problems) in Cuba, he would also be identified by Velázquez as a man to help him with even bolder moves in the New World. However, these bold moves would eventually set Cortés and his commander against each other.

Chapter 2

Tempest in the Carribbean

There's an old adage: "It's not what you know, it's who you know." This means that relationships can often lead to opportunity. It's certainly true today, but it was also true during Cortés's time, as his relationship with Velázquez led to the

Cortés served as secretary to Diego Velázquez, who inspired Cortés with his ruthless campaigns on the islands of Hispaniola and Cuba.

opportunity to explore and conquer Mexico. However, before they got to that point, the two men had a complicated and often quarrelsome relationship. Even after Velázquez gave Cortés the opportunity, the relationship would deteriorate yet again, leading to skirmishes between opposing Spanish forces in Mexico.

Understanding the conflict between Cortés and Velázquez is crucial to understanding much of what happened later. It may well have driven Cortés to take many of the risks he took in America. Yet Velázquez's choice of Cortés is a mysterious one. It is unknown why he would choose a man he had struggled against for years to command such a vital mission of exploration.

A Complicated Relationships with the Xuarez Family

The origin of the feud between Cortés and Velázquez lay in their relationships with the Xuarez family. The family, consisting of Juan Xuarez, his sister, whose name was unrecorded, and her two daughters, Catalina and Leonor, had immigrated to the West Indies from Spain in 1509.

The two girls were ladies-in-waiting to Doña Maria de Cuellar. She herself was a lady-in-waiting to Maria de Toledo, wife of Diego Columbus, Christopher Columbus's son who was the **viceroy** of the Indies. Diego Velázquez became engaged to Maria de Cuellar while she lived in Santo Domingo. After Velázquez conquered Cuba, de Cuellar moved there to marry him. The Xuarez family accompanied her to the new colony.

Catalina Xuarez was very beautiful, and she caught the eye of Cortés, who, at the time, was a successful businessman in Cuba. His service to Velázquez had been rewarded with one of the best estates on the island. Gold had been discovered on his land, and Cortés was beginning to build a fortune. Soon Cortés started

Hernán Cortés

Cortés courted Catalina Xuarez, the beautiful daughter of Spanish immigrants to the West Indies.

a relationship with Catalina. Meanwhile, Maria de Cuellar had died not long after marrying Velázquez. After her death, Velázquez became involved with Catalina's sister, Leonor.

Historians are uncertain about how these events unfolded. They believe that Cortés's relationship with Catalina had become more serious, prompting the young woman to expect a marriage proposal from her suitor. For reasons that are unknown, Cortés refused to propose, a shocking breach of courtesy for the day, which made Velázquez dislike him for shaming the family of the woman with whom he was romantically linked. To worsen matters, Cortés openly made himself an enemy of the powerful Cuban governor.

As was his right as the commander of the expedition that had conquered the island, Velázquez had handed out estates to the Spanish soldiers who had accompanied him based on his personal whim. Cortés, who had done well for himself, had no complaints about these actions, as other men did. They wanted to appeal the division of land to a panel of judges recently sent to Hispaniola to oversee the Spanish colonies. They wrote letters and acquired documents that they felt proved that Velázquez had been unfair. Specifically, they felt that the land given to the Spaniards had been distributed unevenly. However, these disgruntled men needed an educated man of influence to plead their case to the judges in Santo Domingo. Their obvious choice for spokesman was unanimous. They wanted Cortés to present their argument before the judge.

A Political Misstep

It is unclear why Cortés would have wanted to accept this assignment. He had not suffered from Velázquez's division of land. In fact, his close relationship to the governor had turned out quite well for him. Yet he chose to risk not only his position, but also his life. The plan, which called for a hazardous trip to Santo Domingo in a canoe, was a dangerous one. Cortés had to face the political enemies of the most powerful man in Cuba. Unfortunately, researchers only speculate on Cortés's motivations. Perhaps he really felt that Velázquez had treated the other Spaniards unfairly, and wanted to bring them justice. This is a strong possibility, as Cortés was known for speaking critically about the *encomienda* system while in Hispaniola. Perhaps he wanted to distinguish himself by arguing an important legal case before the judges in Santo Domingo. Or, perhaps he interpreted the unrest of the other Spaniards as a sign that Velázquez's power in Cuba was weakening. This may be the most likely explanation, for Cortés had an uncanny instinct for knowing when a person's position had weakened, and when to move against him.

However, in this particular case, Cortés's cunning instincts were wrong. Velázquez somehow found out what Cortés was planning and had him arrested. The two men, once companions and friends, were now bitter enemies. To make matters worse for Cortés, Catalina was suing him for breach of contract, for failing to marry her after promising that he would. Still acting as the governor of Cuba, Velázquez ordered Cortés placed in the **stocks**, where he would have been publicly ridiculed. The wily Cortés was not yet beaten, though.

Escaping the Stocks

Somehow Cortés escaped from the stocks, either by prying open the lock or bribing his guards. Fleeing Velázquez's men, he took refuge in a church and asked for **sanctuary**. This was a

When Cortés was arrested for conspiring against Velázquez, he was placed in stocks much like these. Placing criminals in the stocks was a common practice at the time.

time-honored tradition that meant as long as Cortés stayed in the church, he could not be arrested or harmed. However, he was soon lured out of the building, perhaps by Catalina, who had come to speak with him, and arrested by soldiers led by a man named Juan Escudero. (Years later, during the conquest of Mexico, Cortés had Escudero hanged, surely seeking revenge for having been captured by him in Cuba.)

This time Cortés was chained and thrown into the hold of a ship that was to sail to Hispaniola. There Cortés would be tried by the very judges he had hoped to appear in front of to attack Velázquez. Once again, however, he managed to escape, almost certainly by bribery, and stole a small boat. Unable to fight the current, he swam back to Cuba, with the documents that he hoped would condemn Velázquez wrapped in a handkerchief tied to his head to keep them dry.

Again he took sanctuary in a church, but this time he made sure to improve his position before he left. Juan Xuarez and Cortés resolved their differences. He agreed to marry Catalina, and Xuarez agreed to drop the lawsuit. Cortés then managed to reconcile with Velázquez, too, for the moment ending their feud. Velázquez even became the godfather of a child Cortés had fathered with a Native woman.

Building His Fortune and Power

In 1513, Cortés was engaged to Catalina, and although he waited for two years to actually marry her, they lived together as if they were already husband and wife. He had been in the New World for nearly a decade and was making his fortune. In the years to come, he twice served as *alcalde*, or mayor, of Santiago, one of the largest towns in Cuba. The headstrong, restless years of his youth were over. Although he would remain an impulsive man, and one who would take risks until the end of his life, he now showed that he possessed patience.

Unlike many of the other Spaniards, Cortés carefully worked his estate, using superior planting techniques. He conserved the gold found on his land, trying to discover the richest veins

A bust of Bernal del Castillo, one of the conquistadors who fought with Cortés in Mexico and recorded much of his experience.

AN EARLY MEETING WITH A FUTURE SOLDIER

The soldier of fortune Bernal Díaz del Castillo, who would later serve with Cortés in Mexico as well as write one of the most important histories of the conquest, first met Cortés around this time. His description of Cortés was a flattering one. Besides commenting on his strong stature, Castillo wrote that Cortés had a "somewhat pale complexion and serious expression. If his features lacked something it was because they were too small, his eyes mild and grave. His beard and hair were black and thin . . . His legs were bowed and he was an excellent horseman . . . when he was angry the veins in his throat and forehead would stand out, and when he was very angry he would not talk at all."

rather than just grabbing what was easiest to obtain. Cortés also became friendly with other landowners throughout Cuba, and gained a reputation as a gracious and generous host. Although he may not have known it at the time, Cortés was laying the groundwork for his eventual successes in Mexico.

Cortés seemed to have fulfilled all of his dreams. Besides owning a rich estate in the New World, he was in a position of power and respect. He was married to a beautiful woman with connections to the rulers of the Spanish New World. Then, in 1517, events occurred that would bring him even greater power, riches, and fame.

Exploring Further West

Strangely enough, twenty-five years after Columbus's first trip to the West Indies, the Spanish had still not explored much to the west of Cuba and Hispaniola. Although there were rumors of a land that might be a large island in that direction, no one had ventured to explore it. Needing more slaves to work the plantations and mines of Cuba, Velázquez authorized an expedition of three ships and more than a hundred men (including Bernal Díaz del Castillo) under the command of Francisco Hernández de Córdoba to explore present-day Central America and capture Native people there to enslave.

They returned much worse for the wear. They had discovered several developments made of stone on the **Yucatan Peninsula**, the first actual cities that the Spanish had seen in the New World. However, the Native inhabitants had attacked them. The explorers had escaped with a small amount of gold taken from a Mayan couple whom the Spanish named Juan and Melchior.

Velázquez was interested in what Cordoba had found. The gold the Spanish had discovered in Hispaniola and Cuba had never amounted to much. The "island" of Yucatan, much larger than either Cuba or Hispaniola, promised to have much more of the precious metal. He authorized another expedition, this one under his nephew, Juan de Grijalva. While Grijalva was gone, Velázquez, worrying that his nephew might try to claim the land for himself, sent another expedition out under the command of Cristóbal de Olid. When Olid's ship was late in returning, he began to plan yet another expedition, this one led by Cortés. It marked the first time that Cortés ever showed an interest in the newly discovered lands to the west.

Cortés Journeys West

That Velázquez chose Cortés to lead the expedition after so much bad blood had passed between them seems unusual. Indeed, Cortés was not his first choice. His favorite lieutenants were either in Spain or unwilling to put up the money that Velázquez demanded as their share of the expenses for the voyage. Around this same time, Cortés secretly met with two high-placed advisers to Velázquez and made a deal with them: If they would support him for the leadership of the expedition, he would split his share of the profits. By now, one of the ships of Grijalva's fleet had returned to Cuba laden with gold. Soon the remaining ships of Grijalva and Olid's fleets returned, too. Grijalva told of finding an island named Cozumel, and of a region called Tabasco, after a Native chief by the same name, where they were welcomed. To the north and west of Tabasco they had come across richly dressed Native people who had given them gold and jewels. These tales, and others like them, increased interest in the new expedition.

Velázquez gave Cortés a number of instructions. He was to treat the Native people well and teach them about Christianity, as well as about the king of Spain. The explorers were instructed not to take anything from the Native people by force. He was also required to search for any shipwrecked Spaniards who might be in the area. Velázquez told Cortés not to venture inland, but to instead sleep each night on the ship. He was to take possession of all the lands he found for Spain, but no mention was made of establishing any settlements. Velázquez clearly wanted to settle the lands, because then he would be able to claim all the territory he found for himself, instead of the viceroy of the Indies, who was his superior and legally entitled to anything found by Velázquez's expeditions.

Cortés readily agreed to all of these conditions, and quickly set about preparing for the journey. He ordered a fine banner, embroidered with a Christian cross in gold thread and the message, "Comrades, in true faith let us follow the Holy Cross and together we will conquer." He hired a crier to go through the towns of Cuba and proclaim that anyone who accompanied him would receive a share of treasure gained by the expedition, as well as a grant of land and Native people to care for it. More than 300 men decided to join him.

He also tended to practical matters. Cortés took supplies such as food and oil; trade goods such as glass beads, mirrors, and ribbons; weapons, especially crossbows, primitive firearms known as harquebuses, and several small cannons; and horses. Cortés spared no expense in gathering everything he thought he would need for the trip, including mortgaging his property and subsequently going into debt. This behavior caused Velázquez to become suspicious.

Whatever Cortés was planning, it seemed clear that it was not going to be limited only to trading with the Native people of the new lands. Thinking that Velázquez would try to remove him from the expedition entirely, Cortés ordered his men to take all the meat they could from local storehouses, and then quickly took to the sea from Santiago in November.

His fleet sailed along the coast of Cuba, stopping to pick up more men and supplies along the way. Velázquez tried to arrest him twice, but Cortés, now coming into his own as a leader, was able to convince the governor's men not to take him in. His leadership abilities, most likely along with a few well-placed bribes, kept the expedition stable.

Cortés finally was ready for his journey in early 1519. His fleet of eleven ships and more than 1,000 men, including soldiers, sailors, and slaves, was well armed with large and small weapons including cannons, guns, swords, and crossbows. They had horses, tools, and supplies needed to do more than just follow Velázquez's specific orders of surveying the coastal cities of this new land. It isn't clear if Cortés had already decided to defy Velázquez and head inland, but Velázquez must have thought it was a possibility. He personally arrived at the dock in western Cuba to revoke the agreement with Cortés. Cortés, however, was able to launch his fleet and head toward Mexico.

Chapter 3

Golden
Empires

efore heading to the mainland of Mexico, Cortés planned to land on the island of Cozumel, which had been discovered the previous year by his countryman Juan de Grijalva. After the reports of mainland warriors attacking previous expeditions,

The Spaniards fought many Native American tribes on their way to conquering Mexico.

Hernán Cortés

it made sense to start on an island that had friendlier people who were more like the original inhabitants of Cuba and Hispaniola. However, one of the ships in Cortés's fleet was captained by Pedro de Alvarado, who had accompanied Grijalva on the earlier journey to Cozumel. Instead of waiting for Cortés and the others, his ship landed on the island early, and its crewmen stole food and gold from the Native people.

Cortés was furious with the redheaded Alvarado, a headstrong young man who perhaps reminded Cortés of himself. Alvarado returned the gold the Spaniards had stolen from the temples and paid for the food they had taken with metal tools and green-colored glass beads. The Native people, who mistook the glass for jade, prized the trinkets even more so than they did gold. Along with the help of a captured Mayan whom the Spanish named Melchior, Cortés destroyed their pagan idols and instead erected crosses and a shrine to the Virgin Mary. Cortés, having brought a supply of wooden images of the Virgin to give to the Native people he encountered, conquered and converted the entire island with little effort.

Freeing Jerónimo de Aguilar

While in Cozumel, Grijalva's expedition had heard rumors of shipwrecked Spaniards who were living on the mainland. Cortés sent one of the Native people there in search of these men, and amazingly enough, he found one of them.

The Spaniard was a priest named Jerónimo de Aguilar, one of only two remaining survivors of a doomed voyage from Panama to Hispaniola that had been shipwrecked off of the Yucatan. The other survivor, Gonzalo Guerrero, had married the daughter of a chief and become a famous warrior, while Aguilar had become a slave. Using more green-colored glass beads that Cortés had sent with the courier, Aguilar bought his freedom from slavery and traveled to Cozumel.

Aguilar became very useful to Cortés because Aguilar could speak both Mayan and Spanish well, and he took over as translator. He confirmed Cortés's suspicion that a land rich with gold laid to the west. In keeping with his plan to reach this land of gold, Cortés decided to travel next to the region of Tabasco, where Grijalva had heard about the region and its rumored treasures. When Grijalva had visited the area, the inhabitants had traded with him without being provoked. Cortés found that their attitude had changed.

Sailing up the Tabasco River with about eighty of his men, Cortés found a settlement protected by a **stockade**, a high wall made of logs planted like posts in the ground. Using Aguilar to translate, Cortés told the inhabitants of the town that he only wanted to buy supplies of food and water. The truth was that he needed neither—his request was actually just a ploy.

Battling with the Tabascans

The Tabascans brought a large supply of food, but Cortés demanded more. Then he asked permission to enter the town and look for food himself. They told Cortés that he must wait until the following day before beginning his own search for supplies. Clearly fearing an attack, the Tabascans sent the women and children out of town during the night.

They were right to fear it, for that was Cortés's plan. He gathered his remaining men and sent several hundred of them across the river. He ordered them to attack the town from behind.

The next day, the Tabascans brought Cortés more provisions. Then, because they had no more food to offer, the Tabascans demanded that Cortés leave. Cortés then ordered Aguilar to read the *requerimiento* to the Tabascans. This was a document that the conquistadors were legally bound to read to any Native peoples they encountered before fighting with them. It was a brief explanation of the Christian faith and a message stating that, as God's representative on Earth, the pope had given all the lands in the New World to Spain and that all its inhabitants must show obedience to the king. If they did not, they would be considered rebels and dealt with harshly.

While most conquistadors never even bothered to read the requerimiento, Cortés, with his legal training, always made a point of having it read. The Tabascans, however, merely laughed and prepared for a conflict. Melchior, who had deserted Cortés, had told the Tabascans to fight well. He knew that the Tabascans had to crush the Spanish now while they had the ability.

The confrontation became Cortés's first major battle, and the first one in the conquest of Mexico. Although the Tabascans heavily outnumbered him, Cortés and his men had several advantages. One of the Spaniards' benefits was their weaponry of steel swords and spears. The Tabascans had only stone weapons, although one of these, a heavy club lined with razor-sharp bits of glassy stone called obsidian, could cause serious bodily damage. Another advantage that the Spaniards had was their crossbows and primitive muskets. While the muskets were not as reliable as the crossbows, the noise and smoke they produced often panicked the Native people, as did the sight of their horses, never before seen in parts of the New World. (Although he had several small cannons, Cortés did not use them for this battle.)

The Spanish were also more disciplined soldiers who fought as a unit, instead of attacking in a mass of individuals as the Tabascans did. However their biggest advantage was their cavalry. Deathly afraid of the men on horseback, the Tabascans

The Native Americans of Mexico had developed highly sophisticated civilizations well before the arrival of the Spanish. For example, the Aztec capital of Tenochtitlan (shown above) boasted a population of 200,000 when the Spanish arrived.

thought at first that animal and rider were all one creature, half man and half beast.

Cortés led his men from the river toward the town through a shower of arrows and stones shot by Tabascan defenders from behind the stockade. Soon Cortés's remaining men, hidden behind the town, joined the fight. It wasn't long before the Spanish were inside the town, with its defenders dead, wounded, or fleeing for their lives.

Cortés ordered a search of the area for gold and other valuables, but none were found. He dramatically cut three slashes into a sacred tree with his sword and claimed the country for Spain. Shortly afterward, Cortés established his own quarters inside the town's temple. Still, he knew that the conflict was far from finished. For several days, little happened. Spanish patrols sent out from Tabasco had small fights with the Native people, although one fight escalated so much that Cortés was forced to use his cannon. The effects were devastating.

His Victory Over the Tabascans

The following day, Cortés marched his entire force out onto a nearby plain. His plan was to confront the Tabascans, who had summoned their allies to fight with them, making their force a much stronger unit. Bernal Díaz del Castillo wrote in *The Conquest of New Spain* that they surrounded the Spaniards "like mad dogs," but were subdued, in part, by cannon fire. His account continued, "Mesa, our artilleryman, killed many of them with his cannon, for they were formed in great squadrons and they did not open out, so that he could fire at them as he pleased, but with all the hurts and wounds we gave them we could not drive them off."

At this moment, Cortés and his cavalry attacked the Tabascans. Unable to outrun the men on horseback, many of the Tabascans died at the hands of the Spanish, who speared or slashed them with their steel swords. Not surprisingly, the Tabascans fled the battlefield in disorder and soon surrendered. They gave the Spanish small amounts of gold, which was all they had, and told them that they had only fought because their neighboring tribes had belittled them for not facing the Spanish a year earlier. The Tabascans also gave Cortés and his men gifts of food and female slaves, one of who would later mean as much to Cortés as any of his strongest men.

Her name was Malinalli Tenepal, a designation that referred not only to her date of birth in the Aztec calendar, but also to her horoscope. According to the Aztecs, Tenepal, also known as Malinche, was a woman destined to thrive in conflict, and who would speak much and with great liveliness. She was one of twenty female slaves given to the Spaniards, who renamed her Doña Marina. She was beautiful, and was said to be the daughter of a chief who had died young. Doña Marina's mother had sold her into slavery because she had remarried another chief. After she was in the hands of the Spanish, Cortés gave Malinche to one of his favorite captains, Alonso Hernández de Puerto Carrero.

Doña Marina, whom the Tabascans now called Malinche (the suffix *che* literally meant girl or woman), was the most important person Cortés would meet in Mexico. Malinche not only spoke Mayan, as Aguilar did, but she also spoke Nahuatl, the language of the Aztecs. At first Malinche translated Nahuatl into Mayan, and Aguilar would translate her Mayan words to Spanish. Soon, however, she spoke enough Spanish to speak directly to Cortés.

From the first day, Malinche served Cortés with total loyalty, as if she knew immediately that their destinies would be forever linked. Without her assistance, Cortés could not have easily spoken with the Aztecs. He would have been at the mercy of an empire of millions had he not been able to communicate clearly

Malinche (center), who was renamed Doña Marina, was a slave given to the Spanish. Fluent in both the Mayan and Aztec languages, she quickly learned Spanish as well. Her ability to translate made her a key part of Cortés's convoy.

Hernán Cortés

and effectively. Malinche was the key person responsible for his ability to understand the Aztec people, and with her help he was able to achieve one of the most improbable conquests in history. Because of her solid loyalty to Cortés, many contemporary Mexicans remember Malinche as a traitor, the woman who gave their country to a foreign invader.

Meeting with the Aztecs

Cortés was now a proven leader. Having led his men in a winning battle and defeating a much larger force of Native people, he now decided to move closer to the mysterious land of Mexico, which he believed held of all the New World's golden wealth. On Good Friday in 1519, he landed at a place Grijalva had called San Juan de Ulúa. Once there, they were met by representatives of the Aztec Empire, of whom they had only heard rumors and who began supplying the Spaniards with food and other items. Unlike Grijalva, who had also met with Aztec ambassadors, Cortés could communicate with them with Malinche's help. He told them that he was a representative of Charles I, the new Spanish king who was also Emperor Charles V of the Holy Roman Empire, and that he had been sent on a mission to speak with the Aztec emperor, whose great empire was known to Charles. This was a lie, but Cortés was already forming his plan to reach the Aztec capital, Tenochtitlan, without having to fight.

After sending messengers to Tenochtitlan, the Aztecs brought Cortés presents of gold and silver, but told him that he could not meet with their emperor because he was too ill to make the journey. The trip to Tenochtitlan was also a dangerous one for the Spaniards. Cortés insisted and politely said that he could not leave the country until he had met with the emperor; the long and dangerous trip would be nothing after a journey of thousands of miles. While hoping that the Spaniards would decide to leave, the Aztecs continued to offer them gifts of gold. However, in an effort to drive them away from their lands, the Aztecs soon stopped giving them food altogether.

Facing starvation, Cortés had another problem. A large group of his men argued that they should return to Cuba. They begged Cortés to leave San Juan de Ulúa. Expressing that they already had an enormous treasure of gold, they reasoned that it made sense to leave before the entire expedition starved or faced certain death at the hands of the fierce Aztec warriors. Cortés, however, had no intention of leaving. He had already violated his orders by fighting with the Tabascans and certainly would be arrested if he returned to Cuba. Luckily, Cortés had an alternative solution.

A Clever Legal Maneuver

Using the experience he had gained during his legal education, Cortés proposed that the Spaniards found a settlement on the mainland. Some of the men who still supported him quickly agreed to the idea and set up a town council, even though not a single building had been erected. Cortés then resigned as the head of Velázquez's expedition, and was appointed captain-general of the new town of Villa Rica de la Vera Cruz, or "Rich Town of the True Cross." As new colonies came under the direct control of the king, Cortés got out of having to obey Velázquez's orders by using this tactic. In doing so, he would get a much larger share of anything the Spaniards gained in Mexico.

No Direction but Forward

To ensure that King Charles would support his attempted rebellion against Velázquez, Cortés convinced the Spaniards to send all of the treasure they had previously received from the

Aztecs to the Spanish royal family. Cortés appointed Puerto Carrero to oversee this mission. From then on, Malinche rode with Cortés.

Meanwhile, he moved the Spaniards to a new site, 25 miles (40 km) away, where the first buildings of the new town were constructed. Then Cortés took a drastic step: Realizing that his plan to go from the coast to the cities of the Aztecs, a place in the high mountains, would never be accepted by Velázquez's supporters, he ordered that the expedition's ships be stripped of anything useful and then destroyed. His decision forced the Spaniards to be marooned in a strange land, hundreds of miles from help, and surrounded by hostile warriors. "Now we must conquer or die," Cortés is said to have told his men.

Soon after, some Native people from a nearby town came to Cortés. They were Totonacs, the people who lived in a group

When the Totonacs agreed to ally with Cortés against the Aztecs, he insisted that they get rid of their idols. His men proceeded to destroy the statues in their temple.

of some fifty cities that had been previously conquered by the Aztecs. They were cruelly oppressed with heavy taxes and other demands from the Aztecs. These demands included those of sacrificial victims, a common religious practice of the Aztec people. Cortés agreed to help the Totonacs against the Aztecs, and marched his men to Cempoala, the capital of the Totonac region.

After he arrived at the capital and pledged to help the Totonacs, Cortés requested their total allegiance to the king of Spain and to Christianity. Soon after, five tax collectors from the Aztec Empire also arrived. Cortés convinced the Totonacs to imprison them, though this would be seen as a revolt against the Aztecs and would bring punishment on them. By doing this he forced the Totonacs to become his allies as they needed his protection. Next, Cortés secretly allowed two of the tax collectors to escape, sending them to the capital to tell their emperor that Cortés was not really the cause of the revolt, but merely wanted to meet him.

Cortés then told the Totonacs that they must get rid of their idols. They first resisted his request, but Cortés insisted, telling them that the Christian god would protect them now. He and his men destroyed the idols in the temple and erected a cross in their place.

Cortés was now ready to move on to the next stage of his plan, and head to the Aztec's capital city Tenochtitlan. The Totonacs were willing to send their entire army with him, but Cortés took a smaller force, only large enough to transport his cannons and other equipment. As he headed for Tenochtitlan, Cortés left a hundred of his countrymen behind in Vera Cruz to keep his first city secure.

Hernán Cortés

Chapter 4

Changing of the Gods

t the time of Cortés's visit to Tenochtitlan, the Aztecs were being led by their ninth emperor, Montezuma. More than fifty years old, Montezuma (also known as Moctezuma) had already heard reports of the Spanish

Montezuma was the emperor of the Aztec empire when Cortés first arrived.

The Aztecs practiced the ritual sacrifice of human beings, believing that the sacrifices would please their gods.

UNENDING SACRIFICES

The Aztecs believed that in order for their gods to remain pleased, they needed to be fed every day. They firmly believed that the gods would become angry or even die if they were not fed. The trouble was that the only food that the Aztecs believed was worthy of feeding the gods was the human heart. Therefore, the Aztecs practiced human sacrifice on a massive scale.

Aztec priests took sacrificial victims to the top of the pyramid-like temples. The priests would then stretch them out on an altar. While several men held a victim's limbs, the main priest would then take a stone knife and remove his still-beating heart from his chest. The victim's body would be thrown down the stone steps to the pyramid's bottom. Once there, his legs, arms, and head would be removed for various purposes. In some cases, the legs and arms were cooked and eaten.

Whenever possible, the Aztecs avoided sacrificing their own people. Instead, captives were killed, sometimes after an elaborate ritual called the Flower War, where instead of trying to kill their enemies they captured them alive to serve as human sacrifices.

explorers, and their guns and horses. In some ways, the Spanish and the Aztecs were alike. The Aztecs were not natives of Mexico either. These powerful warriors had come from the North and conquered the area and its peoples. The Aztecs had built a grand capital city on an island in the middle of a lake. In addition to being a great military leader, Moctezuma was also the head priest of the Aztec faith, and the religion's rites and rituals were a key aspect of daily life.

The chief god of the Aztecs was known as Huitzilopochtli, which literally means "left-handed hummingbird." According to the Aztecs, this god had many forms, including the god of war. They believed that the gods controlled everything in the universe, including the rising and setting of the sun and the success or failure of crops.

The Aztecs had many other gods. The second most important was **Quetzalcoatl**, which translates in Nahuatl to "feathered serpent." According to legend, he was a bearded man with pale skin who had lived among the Toltecs, whose heirs the Aztecs claimed to be, as the king of the city of Tula. Quetzalcoatl hated human sacrifice, which put him at odds with the other gods. While the Aztec legend claimed that he had been forced to leave for a country across the ocean in the east, he promised one day to return.

An Envoy from the East

When news of a strange, pale-skinned, bearded man who had come across the water with many seemingly magical weapons and animals reached Montezuma, he was troubled. He questioned his advisors. Was this Quetzalcoatl, returning to seek his vengeance on the gods who had exiled him? According to Aztec prophecy, this would mean the end of the empire. Since he was not certain if Cortés was a god or not, Montezuma hesitated, refusing to send his army to crush him while it was still possible. It was in this way that the road for the conquest of the Aztec Empire was opened.

Cortés and his men marched through the coastal jungles and into the mountains of central Mexico. The air grew cooler as they ascended, and snow was visible on the mountain peaks. They came upon the Aztec city of Xocotla, where they were treated rudely. The Aztecs of the city said that they should head for the important religious center of Cholula, but the Totonac guides traveling with Cortés said that he should instead head for Tlaxcala, an independent kingdom that had long fought against the Aztecs. Cortés took their advice, hoping to again reinforce his army, and marched for Tlaxcala.

Along the way, they were attacked several times by the Tlaxcalans, who feared these strangers as much as they feared the

Many Aztecs wondered if Cortés was actually the god Quetzalcoatl.

Aztecs. The battles were fierce, with as many as 40,000 Tlaxcalans attacking the Spaniards, who numbered fewer than 400 men. Still, the Spanish cavalry and cannons proved to be too much for the Tlaxcalans, who were easily defeated. They then invited Cortés and his men to come into their city.

Cortés, who wrote several letters to King Charles, described the religious city, saying that it was "much larger than Granada [one of the most important cities in Spain], and very much stronger, with as good buildings and many more people." While Cortés was in Tlaxcala, Montezuma again sent him gold and treasure, and promised to give the Spanish king tribute (taxes) in slaves and gold every year. He also ordered Cortés to leave and not continue on his path to Tenochtitlan.

Cortés again politely refused. He wanted to meet Montezuma face to face. Feeling stronger and more powerful than ever, Cortés was now beginning to make powerful allies. In addition to the Totonacs, who were rebelling against the Aztecs, he had also subdued the Tlaxcalans, who had never been defeated by the Aztecs and who were now siding with the Spanish. The Tlaxcalans assembled an army of some 100,000 men and began to follow Cortés to the Aztec capital.

Through the Temple of Quetzalcoatl

With his ever-increasing troops behind him, Cortés pressed on to Cholula, a sizeable city that was home to an enormous, breathtaking temple of the god Quetzalcoatl. He and his men were received amicably at first. The residents welcomed the Spaniards with food, and even let them sleep inside the Cholulan palaces. He believed this to be a positive sign that he was making progress toward his ultimate goal. The exploration was making him a great leader with each encounter.

The kindness and generosity at Cholula, however, was not offered to the Spaniards so that they could make an extended stay. Several days went by, and the hosts of these strangers took measures to send a clear message for eviction. The roofs of their houses were flat, and had the higher vantage point. That was where the Cholulans amassed piles of stones to be used in defense of the occupying army. Malinche spotted this crude form of weaponry and reported it to Cortés by nightfall. Hernán Cortés responded with a tactic that can only be called butchery.

The next morning, thousands of Cholulans arrived in the courtyard of the palace where the Spaniards dozed. Although it was later claimed that many of Cortés's men were armed, historians do not know if this is true. What is known is that Cortés had the courtyard sealed, and then led his men in a bloody massacre of the trapped Cholulans. His Tlaxcalan allies, whom he had ordered to remain outside the city, heard the cannon and musket fire, and attacked the town themselves, looting and burning everything in their path. Approximately 3,000 Cholulans died that day, a bloody indication of the fate of anyone who attempted to resist the Spanish takeover.

The Spanish remained in Cholula for a short time before heading to the Valley of Mexico. They passed the huge volcano Popocatepetl, which was erupting, an event the Aztecs took as an omen of bad times to come. Then, from the mountain heights, they beheld the beautiful Valley of Mexico. Far below them, around the large, marshy Lake Texcoco, were many cities of stone, magnificent even from this great distance. There was a large island in the lake, connected to the shore by **causeways** that crossed the shallow regions of the water. Tenochtitlan was the largest and most beautiful of the Aztec cities, glittering white in the sunlight.

As they began to descend into the valley, an emissary from Montezuma again met them. It was the emperor's nephew, Cacama, and he had a message. He urged the Spanish to leave the region. Cortés, never wavering, refused once more, saying he must meet Montezuma.

On November 8, 1519, a righteous and confident Cortés led his men to Tenochtitlan. The causeway was wide enough for four horsemen, but there were frequent gaps in the path, bridged over with wooden boards that could be removed to allow canoes to sail through—or to cut off the capital from the shore. Crossbowmen and musketeers followed the horsemen, many clad in quilted cotton armor, sufficient to stop arrows or stones. In a procession behind them came the Tlaxcalan army.

At a fortress on the way, Montezuma and his court met Cortés and his soldiers. The emperor approached the conquistador on shoes of gold. Cortés tried to embrace him, but was prevented from touching his sacred body. Finally, Montezuma invited Cortés to enter the spectacular city.

Capturing Montezuma

Cortés's months of planning and manipulation had at last allowed him an entrance to the capital of the Aztec Empire without a battle. Montezuma gave Cortés and his men his father's palace as their quarters, as well as many servants and gifts of gold.

The Spanish marveled at the wealth of Tenochtitlan. The great market of Tlatelolco was larger than any in Spain, and sold strange imported goods, foods, and spices from every corner of the empire. The houses were well built, and the city, cleaner than those in Europe, was crisscrossed with many canals that served to transport goods to and from the capital. Cortés also noticed the lovely hanging gardens of the city and remarked about their unusual beauty.

He asked Montezuma to take him to the top of the huge pyramid that was the Aztecs' main religious temple. Once there he examined their idols, which were covered in human blood. Cortés asked if he might erect a Christian cross and a shrine to the Virgin Mary inside the temples so Montezuma could then see which god was most powerful. The emperor simply refused. He threw the Spaniards out, staying behind to make a sacrifice to the gods to apologize for Cortés's insult.

Cortés was constantly troubled by the danger his men faced. He knew they were trapped inside Tenochtitlan, now without any ships to escape. The Spaniards were relying on the Aztecs for their food, and could easily be attacked at any time. With his usual boldness, Cortés devised a plan that was both shocking and laughable: Cortés wanted to take Montezuma as his hostage.

Cortés went to the emperor with four of his most trusted men, including Bernal Díaz del Castillo, and requested that the Aztec leader come to stay at Montezuma's father's palace. Montezuma was outraged, but realizing that Cortés's men were ready to kill him immediately, Montezuma offered instead to give Cortés one of his sons as a hostage.

Cortés dismissed the idea. Surely, he said, there would be nothing wrong with the emperor staying in the house of his own father, close by his foreign guests. Montezuma, astonishingly, agreed to come. Perhaps he felt that fate was closing in on him, and that Cortés really had come to punish the Aztec people, or maybe he had simply given up. At any rate, from that moment forward, Montezuma was a Spanish prisoner.

Ruling the Aztecs Through Montezuma

Cortés, by holding Montezuma captive, had practically become the ruler of the Aztec Empire already, although he issued all of his commands in Montezuma's name. He even struck sacred Aztec idols with an iron bar, enraging the priests. Cortés also took Native rebels from the coast and burned them at the stake in Tenochtitlan's main square. These incidents seem to have roused the imprisoned emperor. By April 1520, Montezuma told Cortés that the Aztecs were turning against him. They were angry that he had taken away their gods. He recommended that Cortés and his men leave. Cortés replied that he must build new ships. To accomplish this, he sent slaves to the coast with some of his men to begin building the new ships, although later Cortés claimed that his intentions were false. He had no plan of completing such a project. Meanwhile, he had sent small parties of Spaniards to every corner of the empire, always searching for golden treasure and profitable luxuries. Then a crisis arose that Cortés did not expect.

His lieutenant, Puerto Carrero, who had been sent in a ship to deliver the Spanish gold directly to King Charles, did not obey his orders and instead stopped in Cuba along the way. It was because of this detour that Diego Velázquez heard about Cortés's attempt to claim all of Mexico for himself. He assembled an expedition of 900 men, under the command of Panfilo de Narvaez, to find Cortés and arrest him. They landed at Vera Cruz in April 1520 and soon began to advance into the mountains.

When Cortés first heard about this new expedition he was pleased, thinking that the soldiers had come as reinforcements for his tired army. However, when Narvaez sent men to demand the surrender of Vera Cruz, Cortés discovered his true intentions. The timing could hardly have been worse for Cortés, since his forces were completely scattered. Leaving Pedro de Alvarado in command of the remaining Spanish in Tenochtitlan, he set out with seventy men to intercept Narvaez. Along the way he was joined by more of his soldiers, but his force was still small. As the 250 men approached Cempoala, the capital of the Totonac kingdom, Narvaez and his men established a camp.

Fighting His Countrymen

Waiting until nightfall, Cortés surrounded the other Spaniards, who were gathered around the temple of Cempoala, and attacked suddenly. Narvaez's men were surprised. Many who were not particularly loyal to Narvaez surrendered immediately. Narvaez was stabbed in one eye and taken prisoner. As soon as he met Cortés, he congratulated the conquistador for capturing him.

Many of Narvaez's men, seeing the gold jewelry worn by Cortés's army, switched sides. This increased Cortés's force to some 1,100 men, including more than 100 on horseback. He also had the assistance of 8,000 Tlaxcalan warriors, and soon it became apparent that he would need each one of them. Cortés quickly marched his army back to the capital, for there was trouble brewing in Tenochtitlan.

Alone in a hostile land, Alvarado had panicked. Believing that the Aztecs were getting ready to assault him, he ordered his men to attack during an important religious ceremony. Thousands of people were packed into one of the great squares of Tenochtitlan. Hundreds or thousands of Aztecs were killed in a bloody replay of the massacre at Cholula. Enraged, the Aztec warriors had risen and forced the Spanish to take refuge in their palace.

Marching Into a Trap

The Aztecs allowed Cortés and his large army to march directly inside the palace, but it was a trap: They wanted only to pack the entire army inside the palace and secure its exits. It had been almost two weeks since the Spanish had been last attacked, but those who had remained in Tenochtitlan were anxious. They had little food or water. The following day, the Aztecs struck.

Days went by and they fought without stopping. The Aztecs fired burning arrows into the thatched roof of the palace, causing many fires. Rocks, arrows, and spears rained down on the Spanish defenders. Several times Cortés sent his cavalry out of the palace, attempting to force their way out, but each time they were driven back. Since brute force failed, Cortés again turned to diplomacy and sent Montezuma to the palace walls to order his people to stop fighting, but it was too late. The Aztecs would no longer listen to their emperor. Stones and arrows were thrown at him, crushing his head. With no desire to live, Montezuma lingered on for three days before dying, all the while refusing to convert to Christianity.

Cortés knew that the Spanish had to escape from the city. He had the huge hoard of treasure they had taken melted down and distributed to his men, although he warned them not to carry so much that they would not be able to move quickly. On the night of June 30, 1520, the Spanish and their remaining Native allies began to creep out of the palace. They attempted to travel along the causeway heading to the shore. They were soon discovered, however, and were fiercely attacked. A canoe full of warriors came alongside the Spaniards, firing arrows and stones at them.

Through the shower of piercing arrows, hundreds of Spaniards tried to escape. Cortés and his men demonstrated enormous courage and paid a high price: More than 800 Spaniards died that night, leaving merely 400 to escape. They had lost all of their muskets and cannons, but they were alive. Cortés, though seriously wounded, had not given up his quest to conquer the Aztec people.

The Spanish conquistadors began to march toward Tlaxcala. Along the way they were attacked by a large army of Aztecs and nearly destroyed. During the battle, however, the Spaniards managed to kill the Aztec army's main general, a result that intimidated even the strongest of the Aztec fighters. After the battle ceased, the Spaniards limped into Tlaxcala.

The Final Push to Conquer the Aztecs

Despite their miserable condition, Cortés's men remained loyal to him. Within several weeks, he had recovered enough to take action again, helping the Tlaxcalans conquer the neighboring land of Tepeaca, a province of the Aztec Empire that lay on the best route from Vera Cruz to Tenochtitlan. Slowly, reinforcements from Spain and the colonies arrived, bringing horses, muskets, and cannons. Cortés began planning his return to the Valley of Mexico.

Since the Aztecs had thousands of warriors capable of surrounding their city in canoes, they could attack anyone on the causeways trying to enter Tenochtitlan. Realizing that he must find a way to prevent this if he hoped to capture the city, Cortés ordered the construction of thirteen sailing ships. These were built on the dry land of Tlaxcala, and then disassembled and carried by thousands of Native people to the Valley of Mexico.

Cortés had another weapon of which he wasn't aware: smallpox, an invisible killer that was destroying the Aztec Empire from the inside. This terrible, disfiguring disease had plagued Europe for thousands of years, but was unknown in the Americas. Many of Cortés's men had already been exposed to the disease and were immune, but the Native people had no such resistance and quickly died by the thousands.

Cortés's plan was to capture the cities around Lake Texcoco and then move on the capital itself. His first target was Texcoco, a city he captured with an army of forty men on horseback and more than 550 foot soldiers, along with thousands of Native

Hernán Cortés

allies. When Cortés and his men approached the city on January 1, 1521, its king fled. Cortés appointed a new king and the entire city sided with him. Many of the Mexican cities were unhappy with Aztec rule, so Cortés used their discontent to his advantage.

While the Texcocans reassembled his ships, Cortés attacked several other cities around the lake and captured Chapultepec, the source of freshwater for Tenochtitlan. (Most of Lake Texcoco was salty and not fit for drinking.)

By May 1521, Cortés was ready to launch the attack on Tenochtitlan. Reinforcements had continued to arrive, and he now had nearly a thousand men with him, including almost a hundred men on horseback and perhaps as many as 200,000 Native allies. Each of his thirteen ships was fitted with a cannon that had been brought by Spanish reinforcements. These ships,

Cortés led his conquistadors and their Tlaxcalan allies in a spectacular attack on Tenochtitlan.

called **brigantines** by Cortés, had both sails and oars. Each carried about twenty men, along with several crossbows and muskets.

On June 1, 1521, Cortés launched his small fleet. The Aztec canoes were no match for his ships, which plowed right through them. The Spaniards used spears and muskets to kill the Aztecs who were thrown into the water. The sails made the ships faster than any canoe, and their cannons were used to attack warriors on the causeways.

By June 9, Cortés and his men reached Tenochtitlan and the attack began. Using the brigantines to keep the Aztecs from attacking from the water, the Spanish marched over three different causeways and were soon fighting inside the city itself, beginning a month of bloody conflict. Each day the Spanish would assault the Aztecs, driving them farther and farther inside the city, but the Aztecs stubbornly fought back. By now, however, their food and water supplies were depleted, and disease further weakened them.

A massive assault by the Spanish on June 30 cost them greatly. They watched in horror as the Aztecs sacrificed some fifty Spanish prisoners they had taken, rolling their mutilated corpses down the long staircase of the great temple.

In a heartbreaking decision that led to the destruction of one of the great early cities of North America, Cortés chose to raze the buildings of Tenochtitlan in order to make it harder for the Aztec warriors to defend their positions. As Cortés and his troops pressed forward, they destroyed buildings and forced the capital's remaining defenders toward the lake. By this time the Aztecs had a new emperor named Cuauhtémoc, but even his leadership was not enough to save his city. Looking to escape the capital, Cuauhtémoc was captured by a Spanish brigantine. The Aztecs finally surrendered on August 13, 1521. Cortés had finally destroyed one of history's great empires.

Chapter 5

The Later Years of Cortés's Life

ortés had captured Tenochtitlan, but his troubles continued. While he had conquered the Aztecs and defeated two of their great emperors, he still had to deal with the consequences of his actions back in Cuba and Spain. By defying his former

Spain's King Charles I was impressed by Cortés, going so far as to grant him a title of nobility over a large portion of Spain's new empire.

commander Velázquez, some Spaniards questions the legality of Cortés actions in Mexico. Not that this would provide any relief to the Aztec people—the Spanish would never provide restitution to the indigenous people. Mexico was now part of the Spanish empire. However, Cortés did run the risk of losing his claim to the land and treasures he had seized in the New World.

Cortés knew that he had been disloyal to Diego Velázquez by ignoring his orders, founding his own town, and marching into the interior of Mexico. Still, he had sent an appeal to King Charles. If the king supported him, then Cortés would be safe from any legal problems.

Getting to speak to the king was particularly difficult, however. Charles was not only king of Spain, but also the ruler of a vast region of Germany and central Europe. Due to his responsibilities to the empire, he spent very little time in Spain. Velázquez also had powerful allies in Spain, most notably Bishop Juan Rodríguez de Fonseca, the head of the council of the Indies and practically the ruler of all of Spain's colonies. He had seized the treasure that Cortés had sent back to Spain and brought serious accusations against him.

A New Position for Cortés

Cortés had troubles of his own in Mexico. He was building its new capital on the ruins of Tenochtitlan while his men continued to explore and add land to his holdings. He also began to grant estates to his followers, recreating the hated encomienda system in New Spain even though a royal decree had tried to end the practice. This defiance would later cause trouble for Cortés. Although he had been opposed to the encomienda system while on the island of Hispaniola, Cortés found that it would be impossible to maintain control of his men without giving them grants of land. As was usual for Cortés, he was certain to keep the best plots for himself.

Thanks to the efforts of his father and other noblemen back home, Cortés was backed by the king and named governor of New Spain in 1523. Nevertheless, his life continued to be blemished by controversy. One of his rivals, Francisco de Garay, the governor of Jamaica, tried to found his own colony in Mexico. Cortés sent his men to establish a town in the region Garay wished to settle. Once he was confirmed as governor of New Spain, Cortés invited Garay to come to Mexico City, where the two men resolved their differences. However, Garay died soon after, and rumors began spreading that Cortés had poisoned him.

Another Controversial Death

This was not the only suspicious death that happened near Cortés. His wife, Catalina, unexpectedly visited him in the summer of 1522. Cortés and Catalina were no longer close and he had fathered several children with Native women, including Malinche. However, he welcomed Catalina with a huge banquet and feast. Within three months, she was dead, supposedly from asthma. The thin mountain air of Mexico City was unhealthy for people with that disease. Nonetheless, many Spaniards were suspicious about her untimely death.

In 1524, Cortés organized an expedition to explore the region now known as Honduras. He chose as the leader of the expedition one of his most loyal lieutenants, Cristóbal de Olid. Olid, having talked to Velázquez in Cuba, decided to take Cortés's lead. He established his own settlement in Honduras and declared himself an independent conquistador, just as Cortés had done earlier at Vera Cruz.

Cortés sent a strong force by sea to attack Olid. Then he took another army south himself, crossing the dense jungles

El ex.^{to} Cast.^{no} camina a las Hibueras

Mexico se redifica

En MADRID en la Ofic
Franco Anno 1726.

Cristóbal de Olid, a lieutenant of Cortés's, formed a settlement on Honduras as an independent conquistador. When Cortés heard the news, he sent out a heavily armed force to attack and kill him.

of Honduras. It was the worst decision of his career. He spent several months cutting his way through hostile rain forest, finally stumbling into a Spanish settlement in Honduras. Aged greatly by his journey, Cortés found that the men he sent to sea had killed Olid.

Then news came that the men he had left in charge in Mexico City, agents of the king sent to help him run the country, had turned against him. Cortés hurried back by sea to Vera Cruz, where he was nearly unrecognizable—so much had he suffered in Honduras. He was able to restore order in the capital, but now he faced even more trouble with the rulers of Spain.

After hearing the many different charges made against Cortés by his enemies, the king decided to conduct a *residencia*, or an investigation, into how he was ruling Mexico. For the next several

Hernán Cortés

years Cortés was suspended from the post of governor of New Spain. Cortés warmly welcomed the lawyer sent to conduct the investigation, Luis Ponce de León. A few days later the official was dead, apparently of a disease that had also killed a man on the ship that brought him to Mexico. His successor, Marcos de Aguilar, an elderly man with a bad stomach, died seven months later. Once again, suspicion about the death fell on Cortés.

Returning to Spain

Cortés decided to return to Spain in order to tell his story to the king. In 1528, he loaded a massive treasure of gold, as well as many strange animals and several Aztec slaves, onto two ships and sailed back to Spain, arriving in Palos in April of that year. It was his first return in twenty-four years.

In the autumn of that year he met King Charles for the first time. Impressed by Cortés's loyalty and clearheaded thinking concerning the administration of Spain's new empire, the king rewarded him richly, naming him the **marquis** of the valley of Oaxaca, a fertile valley that stretched across central Mexico. Cortés was now lord of an area about one-fourth the size of Spain itself. However, King Charles refused to restore Cortés to the governorship of New Spain.

Cortés stayed in Spain until 1530, marrying again, this time a beautiful noblewoman, Doña Juana de Zúñiga. Their marriage was happy and they had a son, Don Martín, and three daughters. While Cortés had been in Spain, a council called an *audiencia* had been established to rule New Spain in his absence. The first audiencia was composed of his enemies, who refused to allow Cortés to enter Mexico City. As a result, he stayed in Texcoco until a second audiencia arrived from Spain. His days as ruler of Mexico were over, in any case.

Cortés retired to the western coast of Mexico. He sent several expeditions into the Pacific, searching for new lands to add to the Spanish Empire, as well as the fabled water passage that would allow ships from Spain to sail directly to the East Indies. (This passage did not exist until the construction of the Panama Canal in the twentieth century.) Unfortunately, his expeditions failed to find anything of interest, although he did sail to Baja California, giving his name to the Sea of Cortés between that peninsula and the mainland of Mexico.

Cortés had sunk a fortune into these explorations and gained little from them. A life of inactivity, however, was intolerable. The new viceroy of Mexico refused to allow him to send out expeditions to the new lands the Spanish were conquering in North and South America. Once again, Cortés decided to return to Spain and plead his case to King Charles.

He arrived there in 1540, but soon found that his influence had vanished. The king had bigger problems than helping out the marquis of the valley. The Protestant Reformation was causing a civil war in Germany, and the crushing taxes King Charles had put on Spain to pay off his debts were causing widespread discontent among the citizens. In 1541, Cortés accompanied King Charles in an attack against one of the rulers of Algeria, but a massive storm wrecked the Spanish fleet and the attack failed before it could begin. Cortés offered to stay behind and attack the Algerians anyway, but he was laughed at instead. Disgusted with his treatment, he decided to return to Mexico, but died before setting sail.

In 1566, almost twenty years after his death, Cortés's bones were transported to Mexico so the famous conquistador's final resting place could be the land he conquered. Several times over the next centuries, his remains were relocated, and in 1823 they were hidden from revolutionaries in the walls of a church during the Mexican War of Independence. A century later, archaeologists found the bones of this great, yet controversial, man. He is now interred at the Church and Hospital of Jesús Nazereno, built on the spot where Cortés and Montezuma allegedly first met.

The Church and Hospital of Jesús Nazareno, Mexico City, is the final resting place for Cortés's body.

Timeline

1485
Hernán Cortés is born in Medellin, Extremadura

1492
The last of Moorish Spain is reconquered by the Spanish

1499
Cortés, some believe, is sent to the University of Salamanca to study law

1502
Cortés decides to sail to Hispaniola with Nicolás de Ovando, but is injured before the journey

1504
Cortés finally leaves Spain for Hispaniola under the command of Alonso Quintero. He is granted land and Native slaves by the governor, and is appointed notary of Azua

1511
Cortés takes part in Diego Velázquez's conquest of Cuba

1513
Cortés becomes engaged to Catalina Xuarez and marries her in 1515

1517
Velázquez authorizes an expedition with more than 100 men to explore Central America

1518

Cortés leads an expedition to the Yucatan Peninsula

1519

Cortés is appointed captain-general of the Spanish Armada, lands in San Juan de Ulúa, and first meets representatives from the Aztec Empire; he mounts an expedition to conquer the Aztec civilization after securing territory he named Villa Rica de la Vera Cruz, an area he hoped to colonize

1521

The Spanish, with Cortés as their leader, topple the Aztec Empire

1521–1650

The Spanish fully colonize Mexico

1522

Cortés's wife, Catalina, suspiciously dies after visiting her husband

1524

Cortés organizes an expedition to explore the region now known as Honduras

1530

Cortés remarries, this time to Dona Juana de Zuniga

1547

Cortés dies in Andalusia, Spain, shortly before he was scheduled to return to Mexico

Glossary

audiencia A council appointed to investigate charges against a Spanish colonial governor.

Aztec The indigenous people of central Mexico who conquered and ruled a large empire. Aztec was the original name for these people. After they conquered the Valley of Mexico, they called themselves "Mexica."

brigantine Any of various light European sailing or rowing vessels.

causeway A road that crosses water. Unlike a bridge, which is built above the water, a causeway is actually built up from the bottom of the body of water.

conquistador A Spanish soldier who explored and conquered regions of the New World.

Flower War An Aztec custom designed to capture people for sacrifice to the gods. The warriors who fought in a Flower War did not try to kill their opponents, but capture them alive.

hidalgo A Spanish word meaning "gentleman." A hidalgo was not a noble, but he was higher in status than ordinary people.

Hispaniola A large island in the Caribbean, site of the first Spanish colony in the New World, Santo Domingo. The present-day nations of Haiti and the Dominican Republic are on Hispaniola.

Iberian Peninsula The peninsula of Europe where Spain and Portugal are located.

infidel A person who does not believe in Christianity or Islam; a nonbeliever; a term usually used by Christians to describe Muslims or Jews, or by Muslims to describe Christians or Jews.

Islam A religion founded by the prophet Mohammed whose followers worship the god Allah.

last rites A sacrament of the Catholic Church that is given to a person who is in imminent danger of dying.

marquis A title of nobility, usually considered well above a baron or lord, and just below that of a duke.

Moors The Muslim invaders of Spain from North Africa.

New World A European term for North and South America—the land that Columbus had "discovered."

Quetzalcoatl A chief god of the Aztecs, or "feathered serpent." Quetzalcoatl was supposed to have once taken the form of a pale-skinned man with a beard; because of this, the Aztecs may have believed the Spanish invaders to be the god or his servants.

requerimiento A document the conquistadors were legally bound to read before fighting the Native people of the Americas. It explained the basics of the Christian religion, and told the Native people that they must accept the rule of the king of Spain.

sanctuary A Christian custom which held that a person inside a church could not be arrested or harmed in any way while he or she remained inside the church building.

stockade A high wall of sharpened logs that is used to surround a fort or town.

stocks A method of public punishment. People put in the stocks were locked into a heavy wooden frame and bound by their hands and/or feet, helpless to protect themselves from the ridicule of passersby.

viceroy A person who rules a region in the name of the king.

Yucatan Peninsula A large peninsula that juts out from the coast of what is now southern Mexico.

For More Information

Books

Levy, Buddy. *Conquistador: Hernan Cortés, King Montezuma, and the Last Stand of the Aztecs.* New York, NY: Bantam Books, 2008.

Serrano, Francisco. *La Malinche: The Princess Who Helped Cortés Conquer an Empire.* Westport, CT: Greenwood Books, 2012.

Wagner, Heather Lehr. *Hernan Cortés.* Great Explorers. New York, NY: Chelsea House, 2009.

Websites

Central and South American Empires: The Aztec World
www.ushistory.org/civ/11.asp
Discover more about the history of the Aztec empire; view maps, Aztec art, and an illustration of the city of Tenochtitlan, and explore links to other websites about ancient Central American cultures.

The Mariner's Museum
ageofex.marinersmuseum.org/index.php?type=explorer&id=34
The Mariner's Museum offers a brief overview of Cortés's life, articles on the locations in the New World he visited, an interactive map of his voyage through Central America, and more.

The PBS Conquistador Website
www.pbs.org/conquistadors/index.html
PBS presents a series of documentaries profiling famous conquistadors, including Cabeza de Vaca, Cortés, Orellana, and Pizarro. By clicking on Cortés (on the Northern Compass point), you can learn more about the adventures of this complicated and controversial man.

Index

Moors, 7–8

Nahuatl language, 32, 39
Narvaez, Panfilo de, 45–46
Native peoples
  death by disease, 48
  relationship with
    Spanish, 5, 8, 9, 13–14,
    22–24, **26**, 27, 29–30,
    33, 35, 45, 47–48, 53
  as slaves, 13, 22
New World, 5–6, 8, 11–14,
  20, 22, 29, 33, 52

Popocatepetl volcano, 42

Quetzalcoatl, 39–41

sacrifices, human, 38, 39
San Juan de Ulúa, 33–34
Santiago, Cuba, 20, 25
Santo Domingo (Hispaniola),
  12–14, 16, 18
ships, 22, 23, 25, 27, 35, 44,
  45, 48–50, 55–56
slavery, 5, 13, 28, 32
South America, 9, 56

Tabasco region, 23, 28, 30
temples, 27, 38, 44
Tenochtitlan, **30**, 33, 36–37,
  41–52
Texcoco, 48–49, 55
Tlaxcala, 40–43, 46–49
Totonac culture, 35–36,
  40–41, 46
trade and trade goods, 24, 28

Velázquez, Diego, 14–25,
  34–35, 45, 52–53
Vera Cruz (Villa Rica de la
  Vera Cruz), 34, 36, 45,
  48, 53–54,

weapons and armor, 24–25,
  29, 39
West Indies, **9**, 12, 16, **17**, 22

Yucatan Peninsula, 22–23, 27

11/16